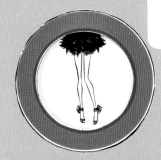
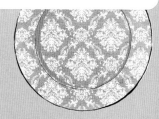

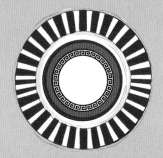

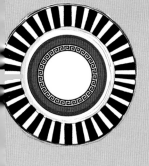

Dankwoord

Lieve ouders, bedankt voor jullie openhartige bijdragen aan dit boek. Door jullie verschillende verhalen krijgt de buitenwereld de gelegenheid te lezen, dat niet één manier van rouwen hetzelfde is. Daarnaast ben ik ook gelukkig met zo'n bevlogen schrijver als Rob. Naast de serieuze kant hebben we veel plezier gehad tijdens het samenwerken.

Bijzondere dank gaat ook zeker uit naar José en Marrian die de tijd hebben genomen om mee te lezen, mee te denken en al mijn ideeën aan te horen en van nuttig commentaar te voorzien. Dank ook aan Kitty en vooral Carla van uitgeverij Scribum. De snelheid, de openheid, het geduld en de directe manier van reageren waardeer ik zeer.

Naast al deze personen voel ik me een bevoorrecht mens dat ik dit werk voor de Wending kan doen. Dat mijn omgeving het accepteert als ik weer eens een afspraak moet afzeggen omdat het werk voorgaat. Dit maakt dat schuldgevoel geen kans krijgt zich te ontwikkelen naar mijn kinderen Lotte, Sjors en Mees, mijn lief en vrienden. Dank jullie wel daarvoor.

Ellen, november 2011

rijk dan ik van tevoren had kunnen bedenken. Die gedachte roept bij mij een mix van enorme bewondering en lichte verbazing op voor al die ouders die dit voor hun kiezen krijgen.

Hierbij past echter één kanttekening. Dat hoopvolle en troostrijke van dit boek zal mogelijk niet opgepikt kunnen worden door álle ouders, en zeker niet voor de ouders van wie vrij recent - en dan bedoel ik een paar jaar geleden - een kind is overleden. Zij zijn misschien nog te verscheurd en gaan nog te zeer gebukt onder het alles verpletterende verdriet dat het overlijden met zich meebrengt. Tijdens het schrijven van dit boek herlas ik onder andere het boek Vingerafdruk van verdriet van Manu Keirse. Hij zegt, vond ik, iets leerzaams over het ervaren van de pijn die bij het verdriet en het verscheurd zijn hoort. Enerzijds doet pijn pijn en is het voelen daarvan een nare ervaring. Maar anderzijds, schrijft hij, is het voelen van de pijn per definitie ook een stapje op weg naar heling. Ook al is het op dat moment zelf niet te merken, en ook al is de weg nog lang. Moge dit inzicht hoop bieden aan ouders voor wie dit boek niet tot troost is geweest.

Rob Bruntink

(*) Rob Bruntink - In het teken van leven.
Zorgen voor het ongeneeslijk zieke kind. Ten Have, Kampen. 2007.

in het hele verdere leven dragen zij de ervaring met zich mee, maar het betekent niet dat er altijd een inktzwarte schaduw over het leven blijft hangen. Eén van de geïnterviewde ouders drukt dat in mijn ogen heel mooi uit: omdat één van haar zoons is overleden, 'zal er aan ieder gevoel van geluk óók een grijs randje zitten'. De verlieservaring staat geluk dus niet per definitie in de weg, al kleurt het de ervaring wel.

Wat ouders na zo'n hypothetische vraag ook bijna altijd zeggen, is dat het verlies van een kind hen het allerergste lijkt dat een mens kan meemaken. Omdat ik van redelijk nabij een man en een vrouw ken die al jarenlang geen idee hebben waar hun dochter is en in feite niet weten of ze nog wel leeft, trok ik die vaststelling voor mezelf altijd al in twijfel. Zou een vermist kind erger kunnen zijn dan een overleden kind? Ook een aantal van de voor dit boek geïnterviewde ouders zetten er hun vraagtekens bij.

Schrijven over ouders die een kind hebben verloren noemt niemand 'leuk'. Ikzelf ook niet. Maar het betekent niet dat het schrijven een sombere, zware, negatieve bezigheid is geweest. Als ik de interviews uit dit boek bij elkaar optel, kan ik niet om de conclusie heen dat een 'leven na de wending' mogelijk is. Niet onmiddellijk en direct, dat spreekt ook nadrukkelijk uit de interviews, maar na enkele jaren gaat men van 'overleven' naar 'leven'. Daarmee is het een hoopvol en troostrijk boek geworden. Méér hoopvol en troost-

ik me daar nauwelijks iets bij voorstellen. Ga je vanaf dat moment als een zombie door het leven? Lukt het je om min of meer twee levens tegelijkertijd te leven: één waarin je de zwaar getroffen ouder bent, en één waarin je die ervaring buiten jezelf weet te houden?

In mijn werk gaat het bijna altijd over mensen die moeten leren omgaan met een verlies. Meestal gaat dat over verlies van gezondheid (bijvoorbeeld door de diagnose kanker) of het verlies van toekomst (omdat een ziekte ongeneeslijk blijkt). De (levens)verhalen die ik van hen hoor, maken duidelijk hoe groot de veerkracht en/of geestkracht van mensen kan zijn en hoezeer men in staat is vanuit die krachten het resterende leven te leven. Zouden diezelfde krachten ook opgeroepen worden als ouders hun kind verliezen? Of is het verlies van een kind van een totaal andere orde?

Wie ouders de nog hypothetische vraag voorlegt 'Wat zou je doen als jouw kind zou zijn overleden?', krijgt vaak als antwoord dat hij of zij dat niet denkt te kunnen overleven. En mochten zij denken dat ze het wel kunnen overleven, dan schatten zij in dat er in dat nieuwe leven geen ruimte meer is voor gewone, alledaagse positieve ervaringen als plezier hebben, genieten of lachen.

De ouders die voor dit boek geïnterviewd zijn, geven aan dat die inschatting maar ten dele klopt. Ja, bijna alle ouders denken aan de mogelijkheid om hun kind achterna te gaan, maar bijna niemand doet het. En ja,

Nabeschouwing

'Ik schreef één keer eerder een boek over ouders waarvan een kind was overleden (*). Het bevat een citaat dat mij in sterke mate intrigeerde. Ik sloot er het boek mee af: 'Na de dood van een kind, probeert iedereen er het beste van te maken. Mensen gaan zelfs hun zegeningen tellen. Ouders die een ziekte- en sterfbed van een kind hebben meegemaakt, zeggen: 'Gelukkig hebben we haar niet van de ene op de andere dag verloren.' Ouders die dát hebben ervaren zeggen juist: 'Gelukkig heeft ons kind geen ziekte- en sterfbed gehad.' Er spreekt een overlevingsdrang uit die bijna 'mooi' is om te zien. Al is dat een gek woord in dit verband. Want er is werkelijk helemaal niets 'mooi' aan het overlijden van een kind.'

Het citaat komt van Ellen Kruijer van De Wending. Juist omdat ik het zo'n hoopvol citaat vond, vond ik het een mooie afsluiter van het boek.

Enkele jaren na de verschijning ervan kreeg ik het verzoek van haar opnieuw een boek te schrijven over ouders die een kind verloren. Ik ging daar graag op in. Vooral omdat het moest gaan over een vraag die in Nederlandstalige boeken nauwelijks beantwoord wordt: hoe vergaat het ouders in de jaren ná het overlijden van hun kind? Ik was erg benieuwd naar hun antwoorden. Als vader van drie gezonde kinderen kon

FASHION HOUSE

For Craig, who designed and built the perfect
home for our little family

FASHION HOUSE

Illustrated interiors from the icons of style

Megan Hess

Hardie Grant

BOOKS

Contents

Introduction

Ever since my first sketch made its mark on the page, I've been madly in love with fashion illustration. Over the years, my passion for illustrating a Chanel dress or Dior coat has never wavered.

But something else has slowly crept into my work and filled me with equal enthusiasm. This is the interior world my fashion inhabits: the rooms that are as beautiful as the clothes one wears.

At first a chair appeared beside a chic woman, then a lamp, and a side table. Before I knew it, I was creating interiors that filled me with utter joy. The interiors I illustrate are much like the clothing I draw; they're imaginary. They're the images that swirl in my head late at night when I can't sleep.

This is what I've always loved about illustration: I get to create an imaginary world, a world where a woman's YSL jumpsuit matches her drapes, perfect pets sit elegantly on sofas covered in tropical fabrics, and rooms become an extension of individual style.

I love to imagine how people inhabit their personal space, where they prefer to eat and how they like to sleep, what furniture they choose and how they decorate a room. A space can say as much about a person as their clothing. This book is about celebrating both.

I've never been interested in creating practical rooms or fashions that suit everyone. I like my interiors the way I like my fashion; over the top, eclectic and filled with drama and humour. The old saying 'more is more' expresses this perfectly.

I hope this book is inspiring and enjoyed with a sense of fun.

As Picasso once said, 'Everything you can imagine is real.'

Megan Hess

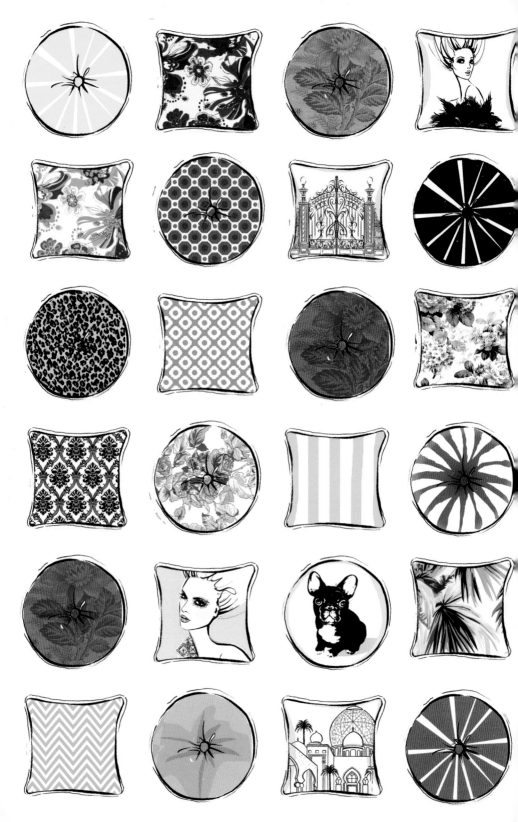

10
ESSENTIAL
PIECES

1

Eclectic Chair

An eclectic chair will always sit proudly in a room,
never matched and always admired.

2

Quirky Crockery

It is much more fun to use quirky crockery than
have it gathering dust in the cupboard.

3

Portrait Piece

Every room should have a portrait piece, if for no other reason than it's nice to have someone else with you in the room.

4

Striking Rug

Like the conductor of an orchestra, a rug is often the piece that leads the other elements in a room, creating a centre point from which the room's style can evolve.

5

Family Heirloom

This is the vintage piece you looked at when you were a child and thought it was ugly or strange, or possibly both, then one day realised it had been brilliant and unique all along.

6

Signature Wallpaper

The options are endless, just choose a design
that makes your heart sing.

7

Vintage Find

It takes a curatorial eye to pick a diamond from the rough
at a second-hand market: it's the thrill of the chase, the
anticipation of discovering that one-off piece that will
transform your home and the smug joy of seeing the beauty
in something that no one else can see.

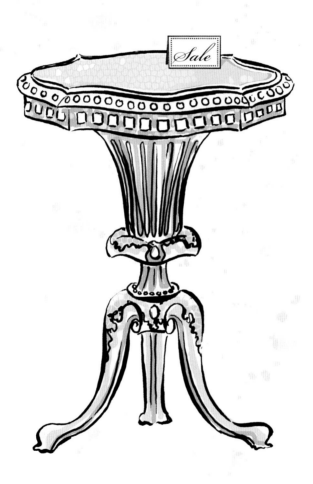

8

Creative Vase

You can never have too many flowers in a home, and the creative vase is an item that began with a different purpose in life but now holds a bouquet beautifully.

9

Courageous Lamp

It's nice to have matching lamps, but the courageous
lamp is one that goes beyond the lamp parameters
and dares to be a little different.

10

Resident Pet

Unlike a piece of furniture, the resident pet will never go out of fashion or clash with the blinds. They will forever rule the roost, and the throw cushions will just have to get in line.

ROOMS TO SWOON OVER

Fashion Office

Carlotta Silk

Lives: Chelsea, London

Loves: the drama of Fashion Week

Loathes: bandage dresses and midriff tops

Wears: anything by Tom Ford

Dreams of: marrying in Chanel Couture

Eats: *Women's Wear Daily* for breakfast

Choose wallpaper with a contrasting pattern in various shades of blue

Framed fashion prints

VOGUE

Muted, creamy tones are an elegant contrast to a rich blue palette

Antiques will add personality and style

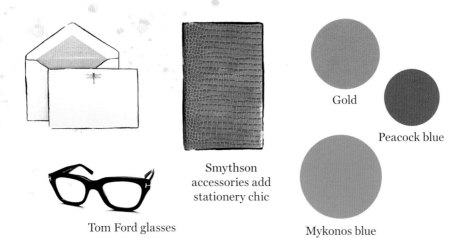

Gold

Peacock blue

Smythson accessories add stationery chic

Tom Ford glasses

Mykonos blue

Fashion Office

Polish the desk and frame the art because this room is for the next Anna Wintour.

A Montblanc pen will take you far

Custom-cover a modern chair in a fresh floral fabric

You either *know* fashion or you *don't.*

ANNA WINTOUR

Grand Estate

Percy Sinclair

Lives: Knightsbridge, London

Loves: visiting his safety deposit box

Loathes: vinyl sofas and amusement parks

Dreams of: purchasing Big Ben

Drinks: single malt Scotch whisky

Wears: Savile Row custom suits

"The details are not the details.
They make the design."

CHARLES EAMES

THE ESTATE

Nothing says grandeur like deer antlers

Graphic patterns and framed architecture prints add masculinity to a room

Choose wallpaper with warmth in vertical stripes

Black velvet single chair

Havana brown

A strong, stone coffee table adds a manly touch

Creamy taupe

Buttery shades are the perfect partner to a rich chocolate palette

Savile Row suits complete the look – pair with flair and add a pocket square

Grand Estate

Hire the butler and buy the scotch because the Grand Estate is for those with classic taste.

A zebra rug is beautiful on polished wood floors

Read the financial papers on a vintage buttoned leather chesterfield sofa

Warehouse Digs

The Browns

Live: East Village, New York

Love: walking their pooch and late-night jazz

Loathe: high-street chain stores and waiting for cabs

Sleep: to the familiar sound of New York traffic

Dream of: opening their own art gallery

Eat: out every night

"It is better to be making the news than taking it;
to be an actor rather than a critic."

WINSTON CHURCHILL

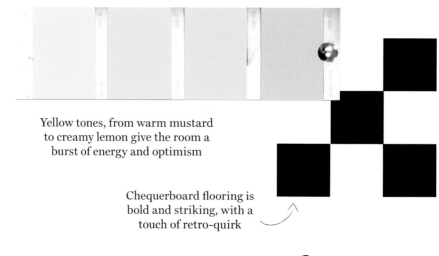

Yellow tones, from warm mustard to creamy lemon give the room a burst of energy and optimism

Chequerboard flooring is bold and striking, with a touch of retro-quirk

Warehouse Digs

Move downtown and create a space that's both comfortable and chic.

Pale lemon

Lemon tango

Choose a statement sofa that is both modern and comfortable

Framed patterns and illustrations add a stylish touch

Select wallpaper with strong geometric shapes

Vintage Tensor lamp

An antique bust contrasts well with modern pieces

The Barcelona chair

ELVIS
WOODY ALLEN
PROUST
HEMINGWAY

NEW YORK

Tropical Escape

Tabatha Polama

Lives: the French Riviera

Loves: escaping to her private tropical villa

Loathes: city air and horrible traffic

Sleeps: on her deluxe hammock

Dreams of: singing a duet with her cockatoo

Eats: fresh fruit for breakfast

"It's kind of fun to do the impossible."
WALT DISNEY

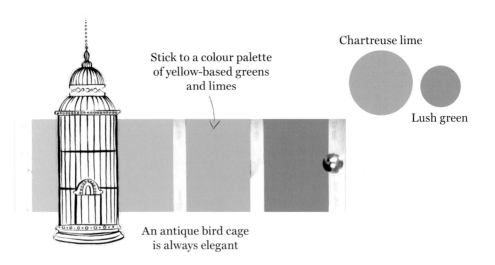

Chartreuse lime

Stick to a colour palette
of yellow-based greens
and limes

Lush green

An antique bird cage
is always elegant

Tropical Escape

Escape to paradise by creating your own little oasis
in lush greens and tropical prints.

Every tropical room
needs a cockatoo

A vintage-style chair in
stripes creates a chic look
that's comfortable

Rich velvet fabrics work well on
traditional single chairs

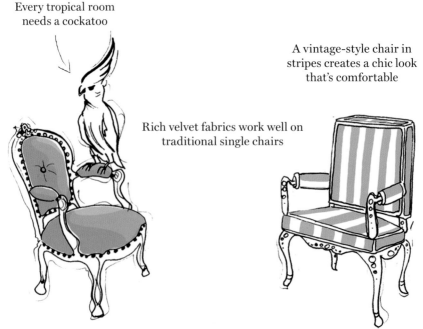

Dress the part in flowing maxi dresses that feel like summer

Frame prints of palms in battered white frames

Choose wallpaper that makes you feel like you are on a tropical island

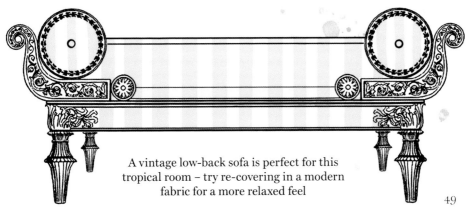

A vintage low-back sofa is perfect for this tropical room – try re-covering in a modern fabric for a more relaxed feel

Distinguished Lobby

Ed and Peter Holt

Live: between Tokyo and London

Love: their cranky but adorable dog, Harry

Loathe: polyester shirts and close talkers

Sleep: to the music of Mozart

Dream of: redecorating Clooney's yacht

Eat: truffles on toast for breakfast

"I have the simplest tastes.
I am always satisfied with the best."

OSCAR WILDE

The large-scale portrait piece is the focus of the space

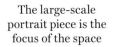

Go for wallpaper in strong stripes or geometric shapes

Dusty purple

Gloss black

Pale lilac

Cheeky Fornasetti pieces take the edge off grandeur

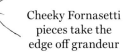

Geometric patterns in lighter hues complement the stronger elements

Choose black accents for chandeliers and lacquered fittings

Distinguished Lobby

Make the entry to your home as fabulous as your wardrobe. Like a classic suit, this lobby is forever.

A palette of purple and silver creates a dramatic backdrop

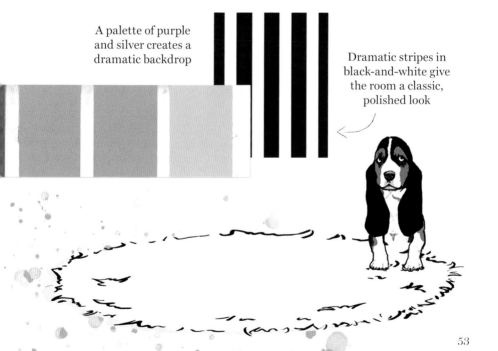

Dramatic stripes in black-and-white give the room a classic, polished look

Vintage Loft

Ingrid Birkin

Lives: Le Marais, Paris

Loves: vintage furniture and handsome men

Loathes: head colds and underwear that rides

Sleeps: in and stays out till late

Dreams of: attending the Crillon Ball

Wears: little black dresses from Lanvin

"The only real elegance is in the mind;
if you've got that, the rest really comes from it."

DIANA VREELAND

Select a rug in a strong
geometric pattern, like this
Jonathon Adler design

The little black dress
is always on-trend

Vintage posters
complete the look

An elegant vintage sofa
in a bold stripe becomes
the centerpiece

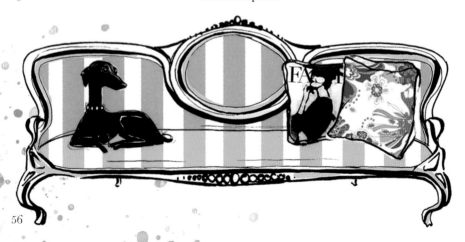

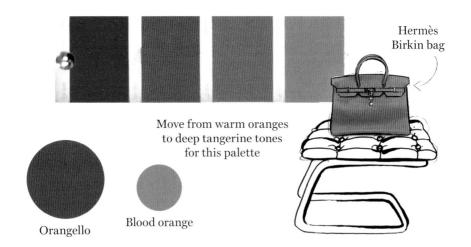

Hermès
Birkin bag

Move from warm oranges
to deep tangerine tones
for this palette

Orangello

Blood orange

Vintage Loft

Just like the fashion editors of the 50s,
this room is built on boldness and style.

Choose a
statement chair

Cherry

A sleek marble coffee table
makes a bold, modern
statement

CHANEL
VINTAGE COUTURE
ELEGANT INTERIORS

Fabulous fashion tomes

Paris Salon

Vanessa Pomp

Lives: 7th Arrondissement, Paris
Loves: entertaining guests with her Chihuahua
Loathes: people who don't like small dogs
Sleeps: with the lights of Paris twinkling
Dreams of: falling madly in love
Eats: pain au chocolat on Sundays

"The word 'impossible' is not French."
NAPOLEON BONAPARTE

Classic pink

Chanel is the
label du jour

Rose-scented
candles complete
the experience

Almost red

Paris Salon

Embrace pink in this Parisian parlour-style apartment.
More is more.

A chaise sofa is a must
– upholster in a vibrant
shade of raspberry

A cream sheepskin
rug is the perfect floor piece

Choose wallpaper with
bursts of floral bouquets,
or garlands of roses

Mix frames and prints
for an eclectic feel

Warm pink tones from
rose to deep red

Zebra chair

Embrace the cliché and
dine only on croissants
and coffee

Eclectic Room

The Fuchsia Family

Lives: Sorrento, Greek Islands

Loves: lazy days and collecting treasures

Loathes: winter and anything grey

Sleeps: to the whisper of the sea breeze

Dreams of: opening a sweets store

Eats: candlelit dinners by the beach

"I love to take things that are everyday and comforting and make them into the most luxurious things in the world."

MARC JACOBS

Hot tangerine

Build a colour palette
of strong rainbow colours

Sorrento blue

Eclectic Room

Mix and don't match in this eclectic room.
Create the space using colour and optimism.

Fall in love with unusual
pieces that bring you joy – like
an original Christopher Guy
Venus shell chair

Sunshine yellow

Louis XV
Upholstered Ribbon
Chair by Dransfield
and Ross

Punk purple

Marc Jacobs
accessories always
add colour

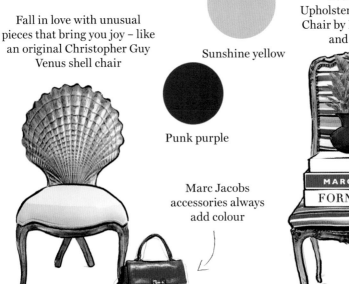

ART

MARC JACOBS

FORNASETTI

Add a beach print to inject
a blast of blue to the room

Mix your art from
vintage oil portraits
to modern prints

Happy Days
wallpaper – chasing
rainbows and lollipops

John Lewis Hayworth sofa in turquoise –
comfy and chic

Gilded Penthouse

The von Trapp Sisters

Live: Munich, Germany

Love: getting together to discuss the family trust

Loathe: bad breath and unsuitable suitors

Sleep: in their luxurious private quarters

Dream of: wearing tracksuits for the day

Drink: chilled Cristal Champagne

"Good friends, good books, and a sleepy conscience: this is the ideal life."

MARK TWAIN

Frame prints in vintage
pewter frames – match sizes
for a classic look

An antique dressmaker's
mannequin is an elegant
addition

Choose wallpaper with
metallic foils for a touch
of glimmer on the walls

Always have
chilled Champagne
at the ready

Couture accessories
are always in fashion

Gloss black

Charred silver

Gilded taupe

Choose muted pewter tones –
silver's more glamorous cousin

Gilded Penthouse

Chill the Champagne and decide on a dress –
the girls are coming for drinks.

Choose a soft silver velvet sofa in a
traditional design. Keep the frame
white for a fresh and modern feel.

Granny Chic

Lara Floraltin

Lives: Tuscany, Italy

Loves: surrounding herself with fresh flowers

Loathes: modern gadgets and reality TV

Sleeps: in a canopy of rose silk sheets

Dreams of: creating the perfect floral fragrance

Eats: high tea at 3pm every day

PEONIES

THE ROSE GARDEN

VALENTINO

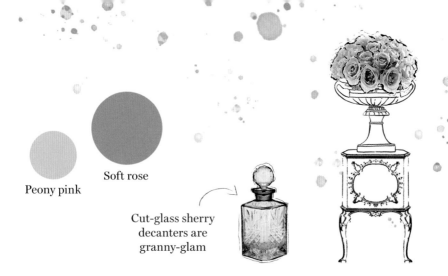

Peony pink

Soft rose

Cut-glass sherry decanters are granny-glam

Granny Chic

Nanna knew what she was doing with all those florals. Now it's time to pay homage.

Ladylike outfits would meet grandma's approval

Silk cushions

Choose a soft, modern sofa in blush linen fabrics

Pick wallpaper
with soft romantic
florals to complete
the room

Select ornate frames
for vintage portraits
for added charm

Touches of white
cut through the
over-sweetness

Pared-back tones
of blushing pink
and cream

Find vintage tables with
Victorian details and
fresh flowers are a must

Mix floral fabrics on
the furnishings to create
a flowering world

PEONIES

THE ROSE GARDEN

VALENTINO

I *hate* housework!
You make the beds,
you do the dishes
and six months
later you have to
start *all over* again.

JOAN RIVERS

Bondi Room

Pip Beachley

Lives: Bondi Beach, Sydney

Loves: coconut meringue and cocktails at sunset

Loathes: tourists and seagulls crowding the sand

Sleeps: to the sound of waves crashing

Dreams of: endless holidays

Wears: bejewelled flats and Zimmerman bikinis

"Never be afraid to laugh at yourself, after all,
you could be missing out on the joke of the century."

DAME EDNA EVERAGE

CHRIS CROSS BUTTERFLY FISH

THE OPAH FISH

COLLETTE DINNIGAN
BONDI BEACH
RESORT STYLE
ZIMMERMAN
TROPICAL ESCAPES

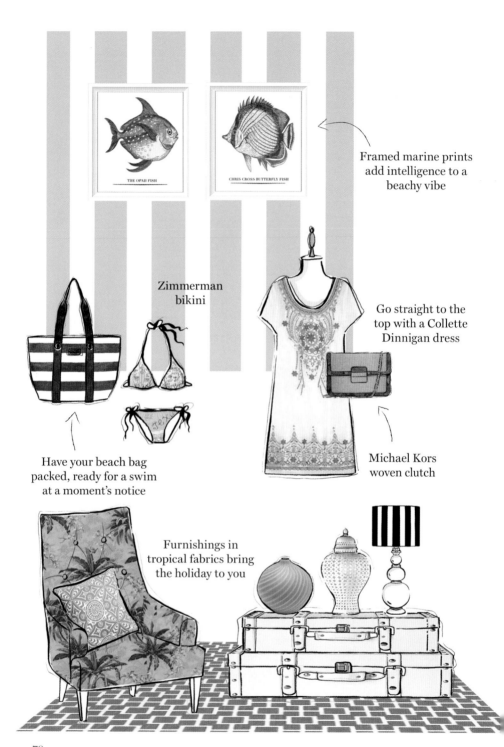

THE OPAH FISH

CHRIS CROSS BUTTERFLY FISH

Framed marine prints add intelligence to a beachy vibe

Zimmerman bikini

Go straight to the top with a Collette Dinnigan dress

Have your beach bag packed, ready for a swim at a moment's notice

Michael Kors woven clutch

Furnishings in tropical fabrics bring the holiday to you

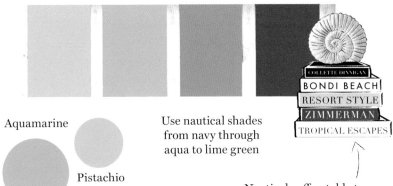

Aquamarine

Use nautical shades
from navy through
aqua to lime green

Pistachio

COLLETTE DINNIGAN
BONDI BEACH
RESORT STYLE
ZIMMERMAN
TROPICAL ESCAPES

Nautical coffee-table tomes
help you stay on message

Bondi Room

Don your designer shades and hit the sand.
This room celebrates your inner beach babe.

Choose modern
palm prints for
cushions

Upholster furniture
in stripes

Art deco
side table

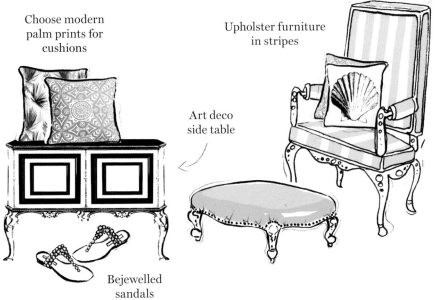

Bejewelled
sandals

Paris Tea House

Carla Panasche

Lives: St Germain, Paris

Loves: indulging in sweets at Ladurée

Loathes: greasy hamburgers and fries

Sleeps: on pistachio-scented cashmere sheets

Dreams of: learning to make the perfect soufflé

Wears: haute couture to buy the milk

Pistachio

Mix creamy vanilla
tones with pistachio
and mint

Gloss black
for accents

Creamy taupe

Paris Tea House

Grab your favourite clutch and head to Ladurée
for the ultimate macaron indulgence.

Sample all
the macarons

Framed prints
of Paris

Antique tableware
is eternally chic

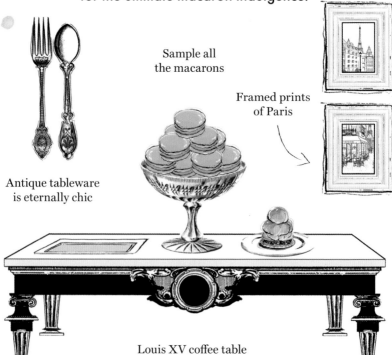

Louis XV coffee table

Forget wallpaper and go straight for lavish baroque panels

Bold stripes pair well with ornate furniture details

Never leave Laduree without treats for later

The little black dress is a Parisian staple

I *generally* avoid temptation, *unless* I can't resist it.

MAE WEST

Palace Chic

The Bathas

Live: Mumbai, India

Love: romance novels and travelling in style

Loathe: rudeness and flavourless cuisine

Sleep: soundly on the finest Indian silks

Dream of: joining the circus as trapeze artists

Drink: herbal tea with a drop of honey

"Imagination is more important than knowledge."

ALBERT EINSTEIN

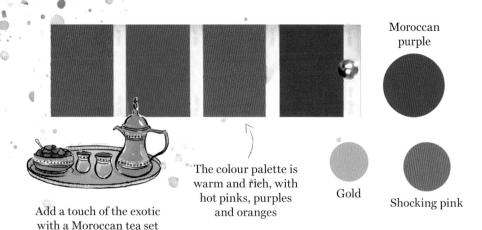

Moroccan purple

Gold

Shocking pink

Add a touch of the exotic with a Moroccan tea set

The colour palette is warm and rich, with hot pinks, purples and oranges

Palace Chic

Rich textures mixed with bright raw silks make this room feel like your very own palace.

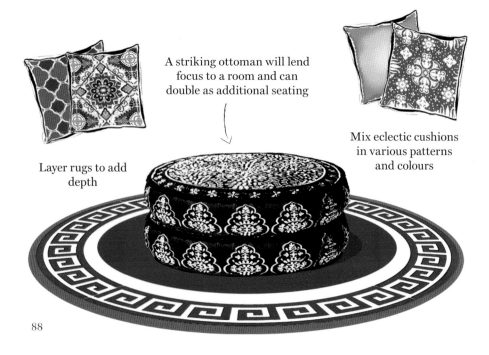

A striking ottoman will lend focus to a room and can double as additional seating

Mix eclectic cushions in various patterns and colours

Layer rugs to add depth

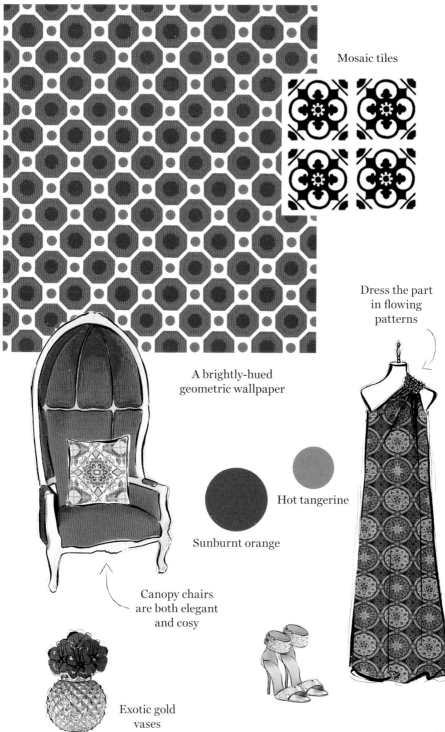

Mosaic tiles

Dress the part
in flowing
patterns

A brightly-hued
geometric wallpaper

Hot tangerine

Sunburnt orange

Canopy chairs
are both elegant
and cosy

Exotic gold
vases

Riviera Suite

Saika Kitagawa

Lives: Nice, Côte d'Azur

Loves: ordering chilled rosé from room service

Loathes: flavourless strawberries

Sleeps: in the afternoon so she can play all night

Dreams of: bathing in peony petals

Wears: silk jumpsuits with killer heels

"Luxury must be comfortable,
otherwise it is not luxury."

COCO CHANEL

THE RIVIERA SUITE

CHEESE CAKES

VANITY FAIR

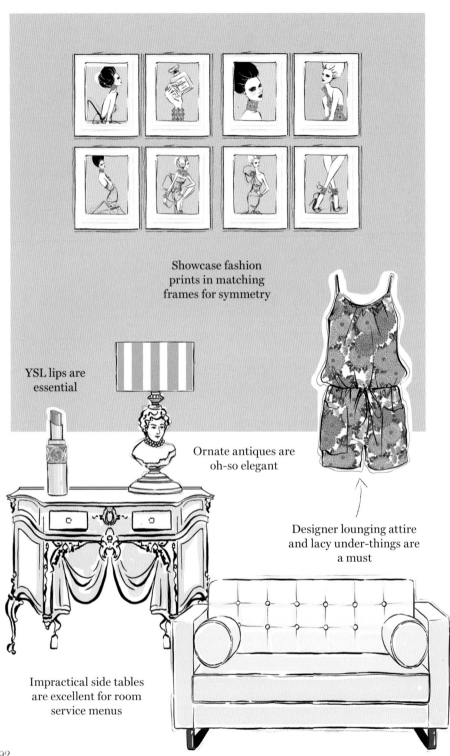

Showcase fashion
prints in matching
frames for symmetry

YSL lips are
essential

Ornate antiques are
oh-so elegant

Designer lounging attire
and lacy under-things are
a must

Impractical side tables
are excellent for room
service menus

Fairy-floss pink

The palette is unashamedly pink, from deep rose to icy fairy-floss

Chantel Thomass lingerie completes the look

Riviera Suite

Get in touch with your feminine side for a room of ladylike excess.

Pale peach

Blushing rose

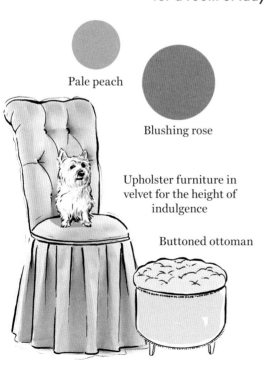

Upholster furniture in velvet for the height of indulgence

Buttoned ottoman

CHEESE CAKES

VANITY FAIR

Only shop in boutiques that use hatboxes

Royal Entry

Esmerelda Toff

Lives: The Ritz Hotel, Paris

Loves: fast cars and trips to Aspen

Loathes: neon lights and tourists

Dines: at the Baccarat Cristal Room

Dreams of: starring in an art-house film

Wears: vintage Yves Saint Laurent

"I used to be Snow White, but I drifted."

MAE WEST

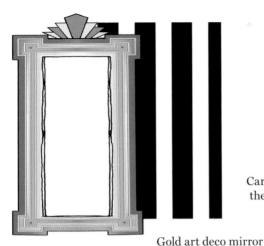

Cartier jewellery is
the perfect choice

Gold art deco mirror

Royal Entry

Think like Valentino and paint the entry red –
nothing demands attention like crimson.

Royal red

Burnt gilding

Pale gold

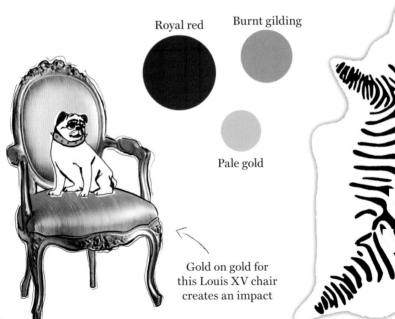

Gold on gold for
this Louis XV chair
creates an impact

Mix wallpapers for impact. Choose a classic black-and-white stripe with a more detailed red vintage design

Frame black-and-white botanical prints in matching frames

Gold tones are the perfect palette to set off rich reds and dramatic blacks

Fresh roses in a vintage gold vase

Accent furnishings in glossy black

A graphic zebra rug anchors this strong look

Valentino heels are a must

Bergdorf Room

Sophia Pascal

Lives: Park Avenue, New York

Loves: brunch at Bergdorf Goodman

Loathes: bad jokes and flat hair

Sleeps: on her therapeutic water bed

Dreams of: editing _The New Yorker_

Eats: Bergdorf's lobster salad

"Each room deserves dignity, respect
and a healthy dose of laughter."

KELLY WEARSTLER

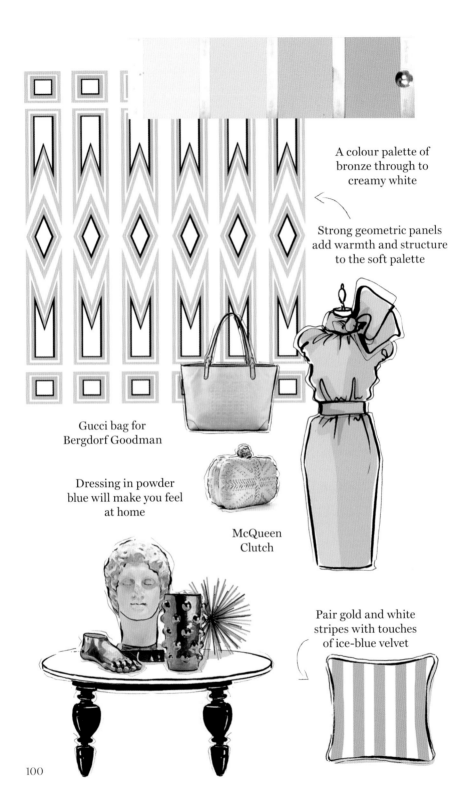

A colour palette of bronze through to creamy white

Strong geometric panels add warmth and structure to the soft palette

Gucci bag for Bergdorf Goodman

Dressing in powder blue will make you feel at home

McQueen Clutch

Pair gold and white stripes with touches of ice-blue velvet

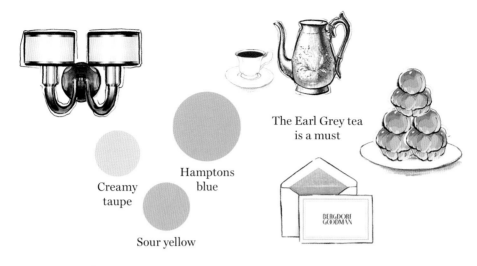

Creamy taupe

Hamptons blue

Sour yellow

The Earl Grey tea is a must

BERGDORF
GOODMAN

Bergdorf Room

Head to Bergdorf Goodman, where the Kelly Wearstler interior is as delicious as the menu.

Choosing the right companion for brunch is crucial – good conversation, manners and a little gossip is essential

Botanical Room

The Honeysuckles

Live: Port Douglas, Australia

Love: deep-sea diving and board games

Loathe: sharks, and sand in their swimsuits

Sleep: in pure organic cotton sheets

Dream of: growing the perfect herb garden

Eat: grilled crayfish for lunch

"Happiness is when what you think, what you say,
and what you do are in harmony."

MAHATMA GANDHI

Frame botanical prints in
weathered white frames

A Dolce & Gabbana woven
tote is perfect for carrying
your beach-ready essentials

Swoon in soft cream
organic cotton dresses

Mint scents fill
the room

Botanical coffee-table
books add interest
and texture

ANTHROPOLOGY
BOTANICALS

A palette of greens
from khaki to forest

A vintage magnifying glass
is quirky and practical

Botanical Room

Bring the outdoors in with a palette of greens
and inspiring plant-based prints.

Palms bring the
tropics to you

Upholster a comfy couch in loud
botanicals for a look that is both
livable and striking

Entertaining Wing

The Fitzgeralds

Live: Upper East Side, New York

Love: throwing a fabulous party

Loathe: unkempt hair and unsocial pets

Sleep: in matching Burberry pajamas

Dream of: co-writing a *New York Times* best seller

Eat: dinner at Balthazar

"I'll always put in one controversial item,
it makes people talk."

DOROTHY DRAPER

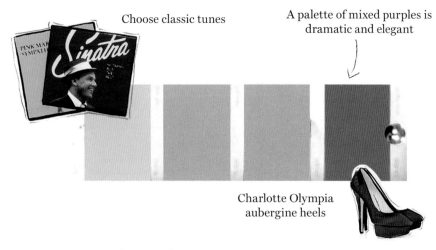

Choose classic tunes

A palette of mixed purples is dramatic and elegant

Charlotte Olympia aubergine heels

Entertaining Wing

Polish the silver and prepare the hors d'oeuvres because the entertaining wing is ready for guests.

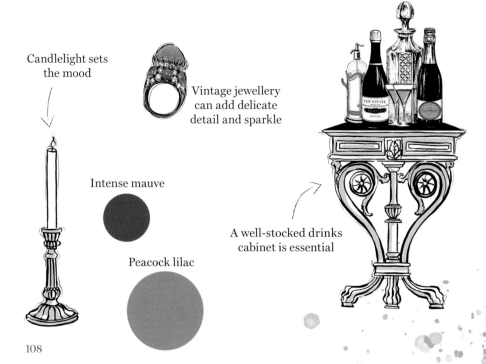

Candlelight sets the mood

Vintage jewellery can add delicate detail and sparkle

Intense mauve

Peacock lilac

A well-stocked drinks cabinet is essential

Showcase fashion illustrations in long, thin frames for extra drama

Select wallpaper in a traditional and elegant damask pattern

A host is part of the furniture – you need to dress the part!

An Invitation

Bespoke stationery

McQueen clutch

A crisp white chesterfield is the perfect sofa on which guests can recline

Savoy High Tea Salon

Lady Hilt & Lotta Gold

Live: Bloomsbury, London

Love: red velvet drapes and hints of gold

Loathe: doughnuts and weak coffee

Wear: Alexander McQueen

Dream of: marrying into royalty

Eat: pastries at noon

Drink: cocktails at 6

THE SAVOY
HIGH TEA SALON

For a striking feature wall, paint molded plaster a rich primary colour

Luxurious furnishings in gilded details and creamy velvet

Alexander McQueen is the perfect attire

McQueen patent leather handbag

A palette of buttery creams set-off dramatic furnishings

Gold

Pale gold

Royal red

A family crest on your tea set adds gravitas

Low light and luxe gold fittings

Champagne is suitable at any time of day

Savoy High Tea Salon

We're bringing decadence back: dress your room in royal reds and gold fit for a queen.

Imposing portraits in gilt frames add regal drama

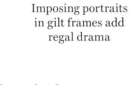

Skip the sandwiches and make a bee-line for the sweets

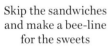

He who placed me in this seat will keep me here.

QUEEN ELIZABETH I

Luxurious Spa

Gwyneth Yelland

Lives: Playa del Carmen, Mexico

Loves: the restorative benefits of bathing in honey

Loathes: wire coathangers and cheap perfume

Sleeps: eight hours a night to enhance her glowing skin

Dreams of: discovering the elixir of life

Drinks: alkalised water

"Life was meant to be lived,
and curiosity must be kept alive."

ELEANOR ROOSEVELT

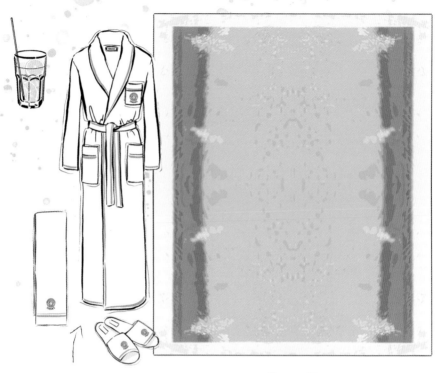

The decadence of spending all day in a fluffy white robe is unsurpassed

Sour gold

Aquamarine

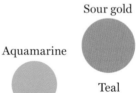

Teal

Water from a golden swan is better for your complexion

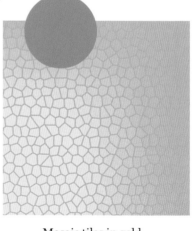

Mosaic tiles in gold

Shades of gold create the colour palette of luxury

Create a home spa with exotic treatments

Luxurious Spa

Life is more manageable after a spa treatment, so bring the spa to your abode.

Be very bold with furnishings, use statement pieces

Scented candles set the mood

Golden accoutrements

White is the only colour for towels

Lemons are nature's detox

Artist's Studio

Megan Hess

Lives: Melbourne, Australia

Loves: Hitchcock films and lemon meringue

Loathes: runny eggs and grumpy people

Wears: vintage dresses and antique jewels

Dreams of: a summer vacation in Versailles

Eats: figs and walnuts drizzled with honey

Elegant officewear always puts a spring in your step

Surround yourself with inspirational prints of moments of fashion history

A comfortable but chic couch is perfect for daydreaming and sketching

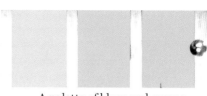

A palette of blues and greens help keep you calm when deadlines loom

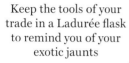

Keep the tools of your trade in a Ladurée flask to remind you of your exotic jaunts

Custom Montblanc fountain pen

Artist's Studio

Ignore the rules and build a space that feels like you — a room in which to dream and create.

Baby blue

Duck-egg green

Soft pistachio

Quirky personal touches add warmth

Writing essentials and sketch pad

Keep essential resources on hand for reference

Happiness
is not a state
to *arrive* at,
but a manner
of *travelling*.

THE
FASHION
SET

Versace Room

Donatella Versace

Lives: Milano, Italy

Loves: to be fearless with a golden tan

Loathes: people who play it safe

Sleeps: on custom silk Versace sheets

Dreams of: peace, love and happiness

Eats: the finest Italian fare

Forget colour and go
straight for gold

Mix Versace cushions
in tones of gold and
patterns of leopard

Choose a white
Versace lamp

Versace Room

Get a spray tan and embrace your inner leopard.
Do gold as only the Italians know how.

Brilliant gold

Bronzed gold

Only an actual Versace sofa will do in
this room – use the colours and texture
as inspiration for the other pieces

Choose a dramatic circular rug

Panelled wallpaper is not over the top in this room

Signature Versace chair

Versace tomes are the only acceptable reading material

A Versace label enables you to get away with wearing gold metal

A traditional round Versace table is the ultimate centrepiece for the room

DONATELLA
VERSACE

Be *brave.*
Creativity
comes from
a *conflict*
of ideas.

DONATELLA VERSACE

Diane Room

Diane von Furstenberg

Lives: Manhattan, New York

Loves: making women feel empowered

Created: the iconic wrap dress

Cherishes: her family and beloved children

Supports: female entrepreneurs all over the world

Helped: save New York's cherished High Line

"You're always with yourself,
so you might as well enjoy the company."
DIANE VON FURSTENBERG

DIANE von FURSTENBERG

DVF

Mix DVF prints with vintage gold mirrors

Mix a base palette of gold with crisp white and bright joyful colours

Diane Room

Create an eclectic boudoir with beautiful pieces from Diane von Furstenburg.

DVF wooden bowl with gold leaf

Colours that pop

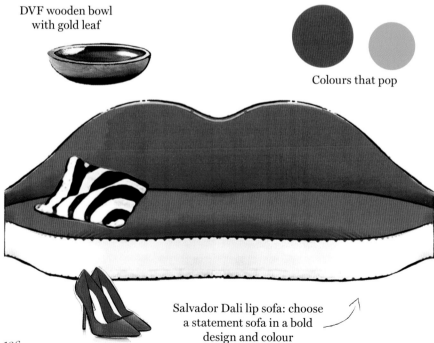

Salvador Dali lip sofa: choose a statement sofa in a bold design and colour

The Candy Kiss - swing it like
Diane in colours that pop

If Andy Warhol did a
portrait of you, then this is a
great place to hang it

Bubblegum pink can
give a sense of fun to
the walls

The iconic wrap
dress in a signature
DVF print

A leopard print rug adds
graphic texture and
warmth to the room

DIANE von FURSTENBERG

DVF

Clean lines allow other
pieces to shine

Audrey Room

Audrey Hepburn

Lived: Manhattan, New York

Made: the little black dress iconic

Starred: as Hollywood's ultimate leading lady

Wore: classic Givenchy couture pieces

Dreamt of: helping those in need

Ate: breakfast at Tiffany's

"The most important thing is to enjoy your life,
to be happy, it's all that matters."

AUDREY HEPBURN

Layer rugs for
interest and texture

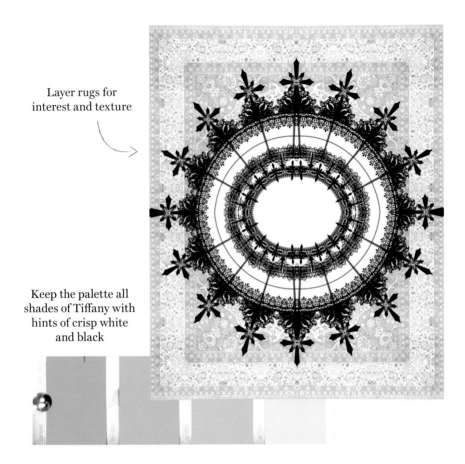

Keep the palette all
shades of Tiffany with
hints of crisp white
and black

The Crystal chair
from Basic Elegance is
perfect for this classic
yet modern room

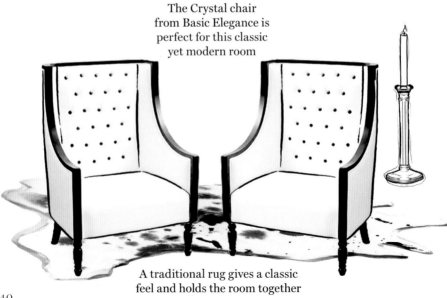

A traditional rug gives a classic
feel and holds the room together

Diamonds really are
a girl's best friend

Little blue boxes fill
your heart with joy

Tiffany blue in
original, dark
and pale

Audrey Room

Head to Fifth Avenue and have breakfast at Tiffany's.
This room is for the Audrey girl.

Not all Tiffany
accessories sparkle

Channel Audrey with
the little black dress

Dalmatians are the ultimate
company for the Audrey
room – scarves are optional

Tom Ford Room

Tom Ford

Lives: Milan, Italy

Loves: walking his smooth fox terriers

Loathes: bad teeth

Dreams of: a flagship store in space

Sleeps: the sleep of the beautiful

Wears: the perfect black suit

Combine strong statement artworks with less insistent pieces, so that neither competes with the other

Lipstick red

Warm gold

Milk chocolate

Alligator skin accessories are a must

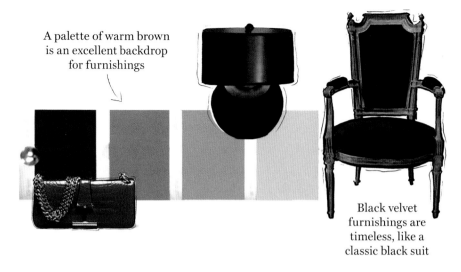

A palette of warm brown is an excellent backdrop for furnishings

Black velvet furnishings are timeless, like a classic black suit

Tom Ford Room

Select the marble and order the croc,
the Tom Ford room is for the utterly fabulous.

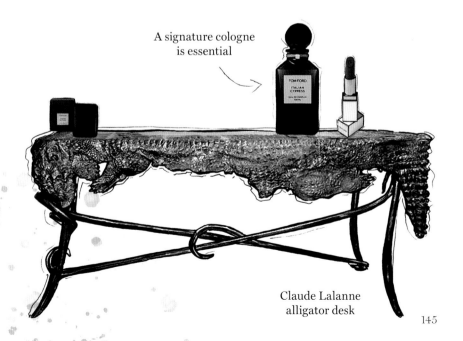

A signature cologne is essential

Claude Lalanne alligator desk

I am not a person who is about reality. I am about enhanced reality.

TOM FORD

Chanel Room

Coco Chanel

Lived: Paris, France

Loved: perfection and silk tweed fabrics

Loathed: sloppy tailoring and small talk

Slept: in her private suite at The Ritz, Paris

Dreamt of: changing the world through fashion

Drank: French hot chocolate at Café Angelina

Only Chanel accessories will
do – either modern or classic

Chanel Room

Feel like you've just moved to Rue Cambon
with an atelier space just like Coco's.

Chanel No. 5: one spritz
and you'll instantly feel
like Coco

Consider restoring
antique furnishings
rather than buying
modern pieces

Subtle tones of taupe work
beautifully with the cream
and black palette

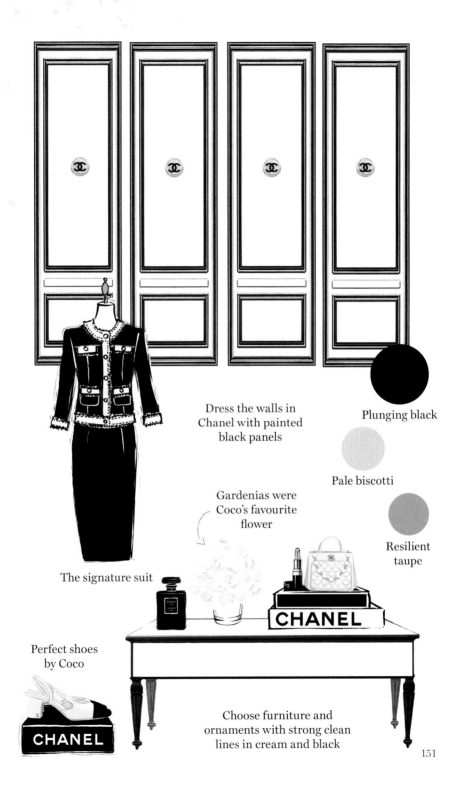

Dress the walls in Chanel with painted black panels

Plunging black

Pale biscotti

Gardenias were Coco's favourite flower

Resilient taupe

The signature suit

Perfect shoes by Coco

CHANEL

Choose furniture and ornaments with strong clean lines in cream and black

I have said that black has it all. White too. Their beauty is *absolute*. It is the perfect *harmony*.

COCO CHANEL

Pucci Room

Veronica Salvador

Lives: Florence, Italy

Loves: geometric prints in colours that pop

Loathes: anything beige and minimalist style

Wears: Pucci from head to toe

Dreams of: kaleidoscopes

Eats: seafood linguini on her deluxe yacht

"I married a Botticelli."

EMILIO PUCCI

Gilt-framed Botticelli busts add instant Italian elegance

A background palette of purples and greens will allow the patterns to shine

You are your room's best feature – make sure you dress the part

Be flamboyant and accessorise the room with other iconic Pucci items

Include ornaments in palette colours to stay on-message without pattern fatigue

A contrasting collection of Pucci prints is an elegant way to play with colour

Pucci Room

Dive into patterns that swirl,
the Pucci room is all about decadent glamour.

Over-the-top gold accessories balance out the vibrant prints perfectly

A gold and white chair offers a moment of calm in a colourful room

Be bold with gold

Dior Room

Grace Kelly

Lived: Monaco

Loved: pale pink peony roses

Inspired: the world with her innate sense of style

Starred in: Alfred Hitchcock's classic, *Rear Window*

Dreamt of: a simple life away from all the fuss

Wore: Dior couture to perfection

"The tones of grey, pale turquoise
and pink will prevail."

CHRISTIAN DIOR

GRACE KELLY

Christian Dior

Dior

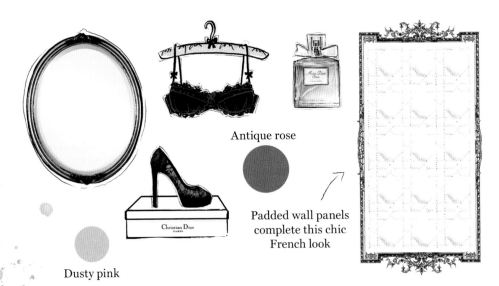

Antique rose

Padded wall panels complete this chic French look

Dusty pink

Dior Room

Close your eyes and imagine a sea of pale pinks in soft quilted leather – welcome to the Dior room.

Choose a muted palette of pale and dusty pinks

Deep blush

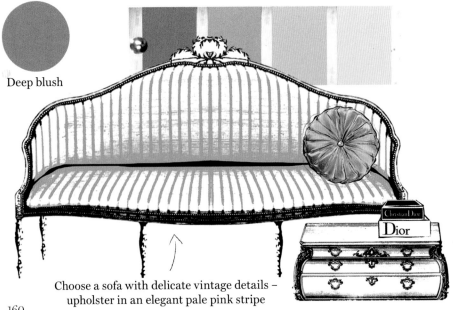

Choose a sofa with delicate vintage details – upholster in an elegant pale pink stripe

Framed vintage fashion illustrations from the 40s and 50s

Mix in a simple but elegant rug

Practice your Oscars speech and dress in head-to-toe Dior

Cover vintage chairs in quilted leather

Lady Dior handbag in signature quilt

Louis Vuitton Room

Sarah Woodward

Lives: Kensington, London

Loves: living the high life in exotic destinations

Loathes: travelling economy

Dreams of: never experiencing winter again

Sleeps: on monogrammed linen

Eats: perfectly poached pears

"Innovation is an evolutionary process,
so it's not necessary to be radical all the time."

MARC JACOBS

Travel in style with dramatic dresses that pack well

Balance out a dark room with an oversized mirror

Framed photos of your travels

Caramel

Mismatched armchairs in vintage leather

Warm chocolate

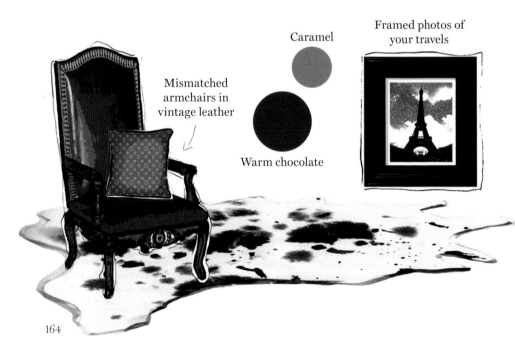

Biscuit

Off-set dark walls
with creamy accents

Battered white
frames add a
weathered detail

Louis Vuitton Room

Pair vintage Louis Vuitton trunks with battered
leather chairs to create a chic globetrotter's lair.

The classic
monogrammed
handbag is a timeless
investment

A Weimaraner is
the perfect resident
for this room

Matching luggage
that doubles as
furniture

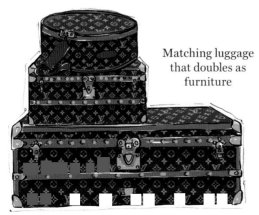

Elizabeth Taylor Room

Elizabeth Taylor

Lived: Bel-Air, California

Loved: romance and bespoke jewellery

Loathed: injustice

Slept: in glittering diamonds

Dreamt of: ridding the world of HIV/AIDS

Drank: Champagne from the finest crystal

"The problem with people who have no vices is that they're going to have some pretty annoying virtues."

ELIZABETH TAYLOR

Don't be coy – portraits
showcasing your beauty
are a must

A palette of pale
blues makes the
red accents pop

Collect a matching
set of handsome
husbands

Elizabeth Taylor Room

No one did decadence better than Liz,
with all-that-glitters and red velvet accents.

A world-class collection
of diamonds makes life
sparkle

Off-white

Ice blue

Always be red
carpet ready

A chandelier adds drama

For the ultimate
statement, channel Liz
with mirrored walls

A couch as decadent as the
woman herself – ornate design
and upholstered in velvet

Cherry red

Serve Champagne in
the finest crystal

Jimmy Choo Room

Tamara Mellon

Lives: Upper West Side, New York

Loves: animal prints and the perfect heels

Loathes: moccasins of any kind

Dreams of: dressing royalty in Jimmy Choos

Eats: fresh cuisine in beautiful locations

Wears: a fedora to receive her OBE

"I want it to feel as though you are walking into a lady's dressing room."

TAMARA MELLON

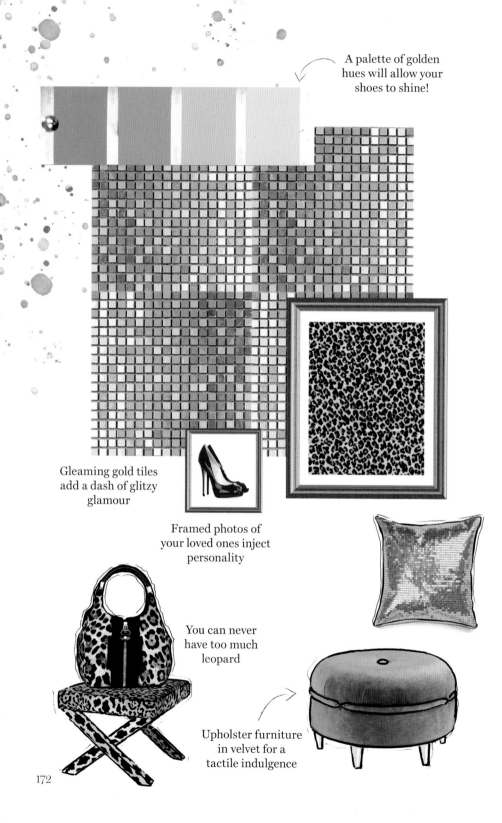

A palette of golden hues will allow your shoes to shine!

Gleaming gold tiles add a dash of glitzy glamour

Framed photos of your loved ones inject personality

You can never have too much leopard

Upholster furniture in velvet for a tactile indulgence

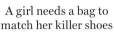

A girl needs a bag to
match her killer shoes

A collection of impossibly
high shoes worthy of
Imelda Marcos

Hot coral

Pale gold

Furious fuschia

Jimmy Choo Room

It's all about textures and colours that pop,
with rich velvet, metallics and a touch of leopard.

The Leon Francois Chervet
desk allows you to always
put your best foot forward

Cire Trudon
room spray

Fresh flowers cut
through the glitter

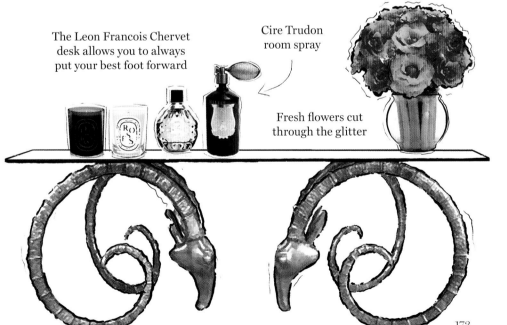

Acknowledgements

To Paul McNally for making this book happen and for understanding my crazy concept and the passion I had behind it.

To Helen Withycombe for being the world's most lovely editor. Thank you for being as engrossed with the details of each room as I was and for making the process of this book so enjoyable.

To everyone at Lamington Drive Gallery for first exhibiting ten of these illustrations and sewing the seed for what was to come.

To Lisa Johnson for your precise pieces of advice. They're like pure nuggets of gold. To Justine Clay for supporting and encouraging my work for many years. In one way or another all my success leads back to you.

And finally, my family. To my beautiful children Gwyn and Will, who can't believe I get to colour-in all day for a living! I can't believe it either. And to Craig, for being my anchor in life. Because of you, I wake up happy every single day.

About the Author

Megan Hess was destined to draw. An initial career in graphic design evolved into art direction for some of the world's leading design agencies. In 2008 Hess illustrated the *New York Times* number one selling book, *Sex And The City*. She has since illustrated portraits for *Vanity Fair* and *Time*, created iconic accessories for Henri Bendel and illustrated the windows of Bergdorf Goodman in New York.

Hess's signature style can also be found on her bespoke range of silk scarves and limited edition prints sold around the globe.

Her renowned clients include Chanel, Dior, Tiffany & Co., Yves Saint Laurent, *Vogue*, *Harpers Bazaar*, Fendi, Ladurée and The Ritz Hotel Paris.

When she's not illustrating, you'll find her scouring the vintage furniture markets looking for that perfect piece she's yet to discover.

Visit Megan at meganhess.com

This edition published in 2023 by Hardie Grant Books, an imprint of Hardie Grant Publishing
First published in 2013

Hardie Grant Books (Melbourne)
Wurundjeri Country
Building 1, 658 Church Street
Richmond, Victoria 3121

Hardie Grant Books (London)
5th & 6th Floors
52–54 Southwark Street
London SE11UN

hardiegrant.com/books

Hardie Grant acknowledges the Traditional Owners of the country on which we work, the Wurundjeri people of the Kulin nation and the Gadigal people of the Eora nation, and recognises their continuing connection to the land, waters and culture. We pay our respects to their Elders past and present.

 A catalogue record for this book is available from the National Library of Australia

Fashion House Special Edition
ISBN 978 1 74379 962 8

10 9 8 7 6 5 4 3 2 1

Publishing Director: Paul McNally
Editor: Helen Withycombe
Design Manager: Heather Menzies
Special Edition Design: Celia Mance
Production Manager: Todd Rechner

Colour reproduction by Splitting Image Colour Studio
Printed in China by Leo Paper Products LTD.

 The paper this book is printed on is from FSC®-certified forests and other sources. FSC® promotes environmentally responsible, socially beneficial and economically viable management of the world's forests.

The Dress: 100 Iconic Moments in Fashion
Paris: Through a Fashion Eye
New York: Through a Fashion Eye
Iconic: The Masters of Italian Fashion
Elegance: The Beauty of French Fashion
The Illustrated World of Couture
Megan Hess: The Little Black Dress
Megan Hess: The Bag
Megan Hess: The Shoe
Coco Chanel: The Illustrated World of a Fashion Icon
Christian Dior: The Illustrated World of a Fashion Master
Audrey Hepburn: The Illustrated World of a Fashion Icon

Claris: The Chicest Mouse in Paris books for children

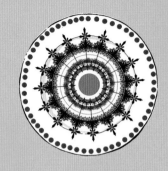

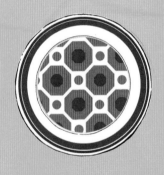